Talbot Stevens is the President of a financial education firm that specializes in teaching people how to benefit financially without sacrificing their standard of living. Whether speaking to the public, corporate staff, or the financial industry, Talbot enthusiastically integrates humour with innovative strategies that add immediate and long-term value.

He is also the author of the bestseller *Financial Freedom Without Sacrifice*, now in its 17th printing with over 145,000 copies sold, and most recently, an educational pamphlet on conservative leverage.

With degrees in Engineering and Computer Science, Mr. Stevens has become recognized for his comprehensive education of *conservative leverage*. Talbot's latest research pioneers fundamental analysis of which investment strategies produce the most after-tax retirement income.

Talbot has been interviewed by numerous newspapers, radio and television programs across the country. He is a contributing writer for Investment Executive, and was a weekly columnist for the London Free Press. Talbot has also written for Money Digest and Canadian MoneySaver.

To ensure that future generations are aware of how easy it is to achieve their own financial freedom, Talbot has started a petition to make basic financial education a mandatory part of the school system. He has also initiated a *"Help a Friend"* campaign to encourage everyone to share valuable ideas with those they care about.

Talbot grew up on a small farm in Southwestern Ontario. He currently resides in London, Ontario with his wife Theresa and their young, tireless, endurance testers, Derek, Ryan, and Kristin. To learn more, visit his web site at www.TalbotStevens.com

"In this clear, concise, and balanced booklet, Talbot takes the reader by the hand and shows how to build wealth quicker through conservative leveraging while avoiding the pitfalls. Any investor – whether large or small – can benefit from Talbot's simple but effective techniques. Don't even think of leveraging until you've read this booklet!"

Dr. Chuck Chakrapani, Chairman, Investors Association of Canada, Editor, Money Digest

"An objective and comprehensive summary of the key issues on a poorly understood strategy. While leveraging is not for everyone, this is destined to dispel the myths of borrowing to invest for both investors and financial professionals."

David Edey, Columnist, Investment Executive

"A balanced account of the risks and rewards of leveraging."

Malcolm P. Hamilton, Actuary, William M. Mercer Ltd.

"At last, both sides of the story. From a source you can trust."

Duff Young, CFA, best-selling author and CEO, FundMonitor.com

"While Talbot Stevens forthrightly sets out the risks of leverage, the probable impact of this ground-breaking investment booklet will likely be to increase its intelligent use by overly cautious Canadian investors."

Jonathan Chevreau, National Post columnist, Publisher of The Boomer.com.

"Whether a financial professional or novice investor, Dispelling the Myths of Borrowing to Invest *gives you the knowledge and methods to magnify your personal wealth over time."*

Catharina Jutting, CFP, Canadian Association of Pre-Retirement Planners

"Talbot dispels the myths about the leveraging process, and offers well-researched conservative leveraging strategies that benefit almost anyone who wants to magnify investment profits."

Alan Caplan, CFP, RFP, Personal Finance Columnist, The Edmonton Sun

"Talbot is a leader in the research and education of advanced financial strategies. Dispelling the Myths of Borrowing to Invest *is the most comprehensive and objective study available on the pros and cons of borrowing to invest."*

Ed Rempel, Certified Financial Planner

"Talbot's booklet on the potential rewards of conservative leveraging is an excellent resource. The pros and cons of various strategies are clearly set out in a format that is easily digested. Conclusions are reached through sound research and quantitative analysis, combined with an appreciation of the risks of leveraging. Talbot clearly shows who should, and should not, leverage. I highly recommend this booklet to anyone who has a serious interest in learning more about this often misunderstood topic."

Doug Greenhow, Chartered Accountant, Certified Financial Planner

"Finally, a book that recognizes that leverage can be a powerful tool for everyone (not just the wealthy) when they use a trusted advisor."

Marilyn Buttery, CommonWealth Financial, Strathroy, Ontario

"Talbot provides a well researched and independent analysis of this important wealth building idea. Anyone serious about building their wealth will appreciate the thoroughness of his research."

Eric Muir, CFP, Investment Advisor, National Bank Financial

"A comprehensive and helpful guide. Coupled with professional advice, Dispelling the Myths of Borrowing to Invest *becomes a powerful tool for personal wealth creation."*

David H. Karas, CFP, RFP, Money Concepts

"Talbot takes concepts often maligned and misunderstood to a new level of understanding in his new booklet. His unique analytical abilities, along with a trusted advisor will help investors to achieve financial success in an area wrought with pitfalls."

Chris Cahill, C.F.P., C.L.U., Ch.F.C., President of
Financial Strategies Group, Author of *Harvesting Your Wealth*

"Started reading and couldn't stop. As a former journalist, I appreciate a well-organized, comprehensive guide outlining the pros and cons of such a poorly understood strategy."

Ron Lindsay Brown, CFP, Money Concepts

"Talbot Stevens is able to show both the positive and negative effects of borrowing to invest in a clear and easily understood fashion."

Michael Corcoran, Certified Financial Planner

Talbot's Summary Booklets
are dedicated to the busy individuals
who want to quickly learn more effective
ways to manage their finances.

Guaranteed Benefit

If you do not feel that you have benefited from the information in this *Talbot's Summary Booklet*, simply return it within 30 days with your receipt to Financial Success Strategies for a full refund, no questions asked.

You will receive a prompt refund, including taxes paid, along with a thank-you for the opportunity to try to help you benefit financially.

Published in 2000 by
Financial Success Strategies Inc.
42 Fawn Court
London, Ontario, Canada
N5X 3X3

Sixth Printing, October, 2005

Disclaimer
Although every effort has been made to ensure the accuracy and completeness of the information contained in this booklet, the author and publishers assume no responsibility for errors, inaccuracies, omissions, or any inconsistency herein. Readers should use their own judgement and/or consult a financial expert for specific applications to their individual situations. Any slights of people or institutions are unintentional.

Volume discounts are available to purchase books to promote a product or service. See inside back cover for details.

Canadian Cataloguing in Publication Data

Stevens, Talbot, 1965-
    Talbot's summary of dispelling the myths of borrowing to invest

ISBN 0-9696873-1-1

1. Financial leverage – Canada. 2. Investments – Canada. I. Title

HG5152.S857 2000   332.6   C00-931997-2

Editor: Barbara Novak, The Writer-in-Residence

Printed in Canada

Contents

Preface

As a financial educator, speaker, and author, I have learned that, for various reasons, borrowing to invest is poorly understood by most investors.

Not being taught even the basics of managing money in school makes it difficult to understand advanced strategies like leveraging, or borrowing to invest. The resulting misconceptions or myths often prevent people from objectively assessing the real risks and rewards of leveraging conservatively as a part of an integrated financial plan.

Most Canadians are quite comfortable borrowing at high, non-deductible interest rates to purchase consumer goods that depreciate quickly. Used responsibly, borrowing can also be a strategy for achieving investment goals, where you pay lower, tax-deductible interest rates to purchase investments that grow in value. However, leverage does not increase returns. It simply magnifies them. When leveraged investments decrease, the financial losses and emotional stresses are magnified as well.

While the *potential* financial benefits from leveraging are quite enticing, the most important benefit of any investment loan program is often the forced discipline that locks in your commitment to your financial future. For some people, the *forced savings* of making payments on an investment loan might be a more effective way of achieving their goals than automatic "pay yourself first" plans that can easily be suspended.

Because of the magnified risks and emotions related to leveraging, working with a trusted financial professional is strongly recommended. Only you and your financial advisor can decide if conservative leverage is right for you.

One of my goals for *Dispelling the Myths of Borrowing to Invest* is to provide such an objective and comprehensive explanation of the pros and cons of leveraging that it impresses and educates the critics. Only by achieving this high standard will *Dispelling the Myths of Borrowing to Invest* be regarded as a valuable tool to help advisors and investors understand and implement leverage in a conservative manner that results in no financial or emotional stress.

With the help of this *Talbot's Summary Booklet*, you can make an objective, informed decision about whether borrowing a small amount to invest in or outside of RRSPs makes sense as a part of your financial plan.

Talbot Stevens

Introduction to Borrowing to Invest

Borrowing to invest is a wealth-building strategy that has been used for thousands of years. The financial term for borrowing to invest is *leveraging*. An advanced investment strategy that is often used by high-income investors, leveraging has also become popular with middle-income Canadians.

Borrowing to invest is fundamentally different from conventional unleveraged investing, and very poorly understood. As we will see, the strategy is a double-edged sword. Because leverage magnifies returns, both good and bad, it can be very profitable when used properly, or it can cause investors to lose more money than they would without borrowing.

Understand and Use the Tool Carefully

Leveraging is like a power tool. Depending on how it is used, it can either help or hurt you. Most of us use power tools to speed up or magnify our efforts, often without enough thought about our safety.

If we use a power saw carefully and responsibly, we might be able to saw ten times as quickly as we could with a hand saw. If we use the same power saw carelessly, without the appropriate precautions and guards in place, we could get hurt.

Why We Use Power Tools

Cars are another tool that almost everyone uses to get us where we're going faster. In spite of the risks, we choose to drive automobiles and use power tools because we want, and reasonably expect, to get the *positively* magnified results.

The critical factor is *how responsibly we use the tool*, whether it's a power tool, an automobile or leveraging. If we use it carefully, with an understanding of how to reduce the risks, then we can reasonably expect to benefit. If we don't, we could get hurt, sometimes badly.

WARNING!

Leverage magnifies returns, making good returns better and bad returns worse. Do not consider the strategy until you fully understand the risks and how to reduce them.

Understanding how to use the tool properly increases the odds of benefiting, and reduces the possibility of getting hurt.

What is Conservative Leverage?

Used aggressively, leverage can produce significant gains or losses. Since no one likes losing money, I have always advised investors to consider only *conservative* leverage. My definition of conservative leverage is where the strategy is understood and implemented in a way that causes no financial or emotional stress.

As with unleveraged investing, there are no guarantees that you will benefit from borrowing to invest, even if you fully understand the potential downside and implement responsibly.

The goal for most investors is to choose the investment strategy that produces the highest net personal benefit for the level of risk you are comfortable with. To make an objective assessment of what level of leveraging, if any, is right for you, you first need a comprehensive understanding of the risks and potential rewards.

The purpose of this *Talbot's Summary Booklet* is to help you make an informed decision by providing an efficient review of the key issues related to borrowing to invest in or outside of RRSPs.

Why Leverage is Controversial

Borrowing to invest is one of the most controversial subjects in financial planning. Opinions from investors, financial advisors, experts and the media vary and conflict.

Much of the controversy arises from a lack of information on leveraging. While there are dozens of books on basic financial planning and all of the intricacies of investing in RRSPs, there are very few resources available to gain even a basic understanding of leverage.

Myths About Borrowing to Invest

Much of the misunderstanding surrounding leverage is related to five myths about borrowing to invest. These myths and other misconceptions often prevent people from objectively evaluating the pros and cons of leveraging in a responsible manner.

Myth 1: Leverage is Only for the Wealthy

One common belief, especially with middle-income investors, is that only the rich borrow to invest. While it is true that the so-called wealthy are bigger users of advanced financial strategies like leverage, this doesn't mean they're the only ones who can use them.

If a strategy can benefit high-income Canadians, it can also benefit lower- and middle-income individuals in a similar way. Although the benefits might be smaller, anyone can act on the ideas of others if they have the same knowledge, attitude, and commitment.

Myth 2: All Debts Are Bad

The second myth is that all debts are evil and should be avoided like the plague. Many of our parents were taught that all debts should be paid off as quickly as possible. This is certainly the right approach for most of our personal debts, like credit cards, where the after-tax interest charge can range from 15 to over 33%. This expensive, non-deductible consumer debt usually results from the purchase of products that drop in value very quickly, and *should* be avoided and/or paid off as soon as possible.

But in addition to this "bad debt", there is also a "good debt" that is often used by the wealthy. This constructive type of borrowing is used to purchase things like investments or businesses that increase in value. The interest charges on "good debt" are much lower, and the real interest rate is usually further reduced by being tax deductible.

Myth 3: Leverage is Too Risky for Me

Many people feel that leveraging is "too risky for me". Leverage risks can be categorized as either financial or emotional. The reality is that most investors who could qualify for an investment loan have already leveraged in a less effective way, with more financial risk, without even realizing it.

When you take out a mortgage and borrow to buy an equity investment like real estate, isn't that leveraged investing? In fact, with mortgages, you can put as little as 5% down. This highly leveraged equity investment generally has poor liquidity, no diversification, expectations for low returns, and the interest expense isn't tax deductible.

As mentioned, people accept non-deductible consumer borrowing as a part of life, despite the fact that it decreases wealth in most cases. Tax deductible borrowing to invest in diversified investments has less financial risk than mortgages or consumer borrowing.

The emotional risk with any form of borrowing may still exist, and depends on your knowledge level, experience, and risk tolerance.

Myth 4: Returns Must Exceed Cost to be Profitable

The fourth myth is based on the very rational belief that for leverage to be profitable, your investment returns must exceed your cost of borrowing. In other words, if the interest expense on your investment loan is 9%, then your investments must return at least 9% or you won't make any money.

Although this is a very reasonable belief, it is generally not true, at least for investments where some or most of the return is a deferred capital gain, as with equity mutual funds.

The breakeven point is the minimum return needed to cover the after-tax interest expense and *start* profiting from leverage. This is where the net gain from leveraging equals the net cost, and hence the profit from borrowing is zero.

Mathematically, the breakeven point defines the financial risk of any strategy.   If we ignore

> ### Definition
>
> The breakeven point is the minimum return needed to cover the after-tax interest expense and *start* profiting from leverage.

inflation and taxes, the savings account that pays 0.25% interest is profitable, even though it would take about 278 years for your money to double.

When borrowing to invest outside of RRSPs, the breakeven point is higher than 0%, but not as high as the cost of borrowing.   One reason that the breakeven point is lower than most people think is the tax deductibility of the interest expense.   The overlooked issue is that capital gains are taxed less and, more importantly, taxed later, compounding tax-deferred like RRSPs.

The prospect of borrowing at 9% interest in order to earn a 9% return leads many people to conclude that they wouldn't benefit by leveraging. But this common myth can cost you — a lot.

> **Example:** If Joe is a baby boomer in the 40% tax bracket and borrows at 9% interest over a 10-year period, he would have to average 5.1% equity returns to break even.
>
> As we will see, earning a 9% average return that just matches his cost of borrowing would increase his retirement fund by about 45%.

Myth 5: Returns Must Exceed Cost to be Better

For most investors, the objective is not simply to breakeven.   This relates to another myth, related to the fourth, which claims that investment returns must be higher than the cost of borrowing for leverage to be better than an unleveraged approach.

This myth, which essentially contends that leverage makes sense only when returns exceed the interest expense, is a commonly held belief in the financial industry, even by many tax experts and chartered accountants.

At first glance, it appears reasonable that an investor will benefit from leveraging only if the returns are higher than the interest expense. However, this is true only if the investment returns are taxed at the same rate and at the same time, as interest. In other words, if the only investments available for leveraging were interest-bearing products, like GICs, where 100% of the interest was taxable each year, then leverage *would* only make sense when returns were higher than the interest rate.

But investments that are largely capital gains, like equity mutual funds, have tax benefits that render the myth false: tax deductions, taxed less, and taxed later. Generally the interest expense is 100% tax deductible, while only a portion of the capital gains are taxable. The bigger tax benefit is the tax deferral. Interest expenses are deductible every year, while the taxes due on capital gains are deferred until you sell for a profit.

Over a long-term period, the "taxed later" and "taxed less" benefits of capital gains mean that leveraging of equity investments is more profitable than an unleveraged strategy even when the returns are less than the cost of borrowing.

Example: If Joe borrows at 9% interest, he would have to average 6.3% equity returns for the net benefits of leveraging to be better than not leveraging. This is about two-thirds of his cost of borrowing.

This critical return, which we might call the "Better Than" return, is the minimum return for leverage to be better than not leveraging. While the breakeven point defines when leveraging *starts* to become profitable, the "better than" return defines when the profit from leveraging is more than the profit that could be produced by investing the same cashflow without leveraging.

It is essential to understand the real "Better Than" return for your unique situation, based on your tax bracket, time horizon, type of investments and other factors before you can objectively assess the potential benefits and risks of borrowing to invest.

Definition

The "Better Than" return is the minimum return needed for leveraging to produce more net benefit than could be achieved by investing the same cashflow without leveraging. It defines the minimum return needed for leveraging to make sense.

Tax Deductibility When Borrowing

When borrowing to invest in RRSPs, the interest expense is not tax deductible, but the amount invested is. With traditional leverage, where you borrow to invest outside of RRSPs, the interest expense is *generally* deductible, but not the amount invested.

The deductibility of interest expenses for non-registered investing can be confusing. The Income Tax Act states that any interest expense incurred to purchase property that produces income is tax deductible. Only dividends and interest qualify as income from investments. Capital gains do not.

If the investment purchased with borrowed money has no potential to produce income in the form of dividends or interest, then the interest expense is not tax deductible.

Some equity mutual funds have paid out little or no income in the form of dividends or interest, and some have questioned whether borrowing to purchase equity mutual funds is tax deductible. The general practice of Canada Revenue Agency or CRA, formerly called Revenue Canada, has been to allow the deductibility of interest when borrowing to buy equity funds. Presumably, this is allowed because any stock, and therefore any collection of stocks, has the *potential* to pay out a dividend. In a similar way, any interest expense incurred to run a business is deductible as long as there is a reasonable chance of producing a net income.

The good news is that the government has finally clarified its position on this issue. In technical interpretation 2000-0036435, CRA states that interest expenses are generally deductible when borrowing to invest in mutual funds or common shares. Segregated funds also qualify.

Note that if you withdraw some leveraged funds for personal reasons, like to buy a boat, a portion of the interest will no longer be deductible.

Investors should acknowledge that the government can change the rules at any time. As of March 30, 2004, provincial tax deductibility of leverage interest for Quebec residents is limited to investment income, with unused deductions able to be carried forward indefinitely. As in any tax matter, individuals should seek professional advice regarding the deductibility of interest expenses.

Borrowing for RRSPs

Perhaps because the interest expense of borrowing to invest in RRSPs is not tax deductible, many investors and financial professionals do not feel that RRSP borrowing makes sense for more than modest amounts that can be paid off within a year.

RRSP Refund Strategies

Before we can assess the merits of larger loans to "catch-up" on RRSP contributions, we must recognize that there are at least 5 different RRSP refund strategies. How you invest in RRSPs, and what you do with the refunds, are important parameters that define your investment behaviour.

Behavioural finance is a relatively new field of psychology that studies why we manage money the way we do. How you view and act towards money can be the most important factor in financial success. With respect to investing, investor performance is more important than investment performance. For example, a good saver can produce a larger retirement fund than a good investor who saves less, particularly for procrastinators with shorter time periods.

With RRSPs, one of the most important factors affecting the size of your retirement fund is what you do with the refunds. This investor behaviour parameter is often overlooked and rarely discussed. Yet, as we will see, acting on a more effective RRSP refund strategy can increase your retirement fund by 25 to 50% or more.

To introduce the 5 RRSP refund strategies, let's consider Anne's situation. To make the math easier to follow, we'll assume that Anne is in the 50% tax bracket, and she has an after-tax cashflow of $1,000 per year available to invest. It is important to keep in mind that we can only invest after-tax dollars, dollars that already have been taxed by the government.

Beyond RRSPs, there are many non-registered investment strategies that could be considered. For now, let's discuss only the different ways that the cashflow can be invested using RRSPs. Each of the following *RRSP refund strategies* defines a different behaviour and commitment to the retirement goal.

1: Spend refund. If Anne is in the 50% tax bracket, and contributes $1,000 to an RRSP, she will get a refund of $500. Unfortunately, the first and most common RRSP refund strategy is to spend it. If Anne spends the $500 refund, her $1,000 a year of after-tax cashflow adds only $1,000 a year to her RRSP.

2: Reinvest refund. As a disciplined investor, Anne knows that she can increase her retirement funds by reinvesting the $500 refund. By reinvesting her refund back into her RRSP, her $1,000 a year of after-tax cashflow results in annual RRSP contributions of $1,500. Simply reinvesting her 50% tax refund increases Anne's retirement fund by the same 50%.

Obviously, any portion of the refund can be reinvested. For labeling purposes, I have defined the second refund strategy where 100% of the refund is reinvested.

While reinvesting the refund is a notable improvement over spending the refund, there are several ways Anne can do even better.

3: Gross-up refund. The third refund strategy allows Anne to increase or "gross-up" $1,000 a year of after-tax cashflow into annual RRSP contributions of

> ### Math Details
>
> To calculate the RRSP contribution produced by reinvesting all of the refund, simply increase the after-tax amount by the rate of the tax bracket. For example, in the 40% tax bracket, investing $1,000 *and* the 40% refund produces a total RRSP contribution of $1,400.

$2,000. Conceptually, the approach is not as straightforward as the other refund strategies. The strategy's "gross-up" label should not be confused with the gross-up of dividends for the calculation of the dividend tax credit.

The gross-up refund strategy produces the maximum RRSP contribution possible per dollar available to invest, without maintaining an RRSP loan. The approach can be implemented in several ways.

With $1,000 to invest, Anne can borrow an extra $1,000 to "gross-up" or increase her total RRSP contribution to $2,000. In a 50% tax bracket, her $2,000 RRSP contribution produces a refund of $1,000. The $1,000 refund is used to completely and almost immediately repay the $1,000 loan so that she pays a negligible amount of interest.

For those in the 50% tax bracket, this approach grosses-up $1,000 into a $2,000 RRSP contribution, doubling their retirement fund relative to the common approach of spending the refund.

The gross-up result occurs whenever you do not get a refund. With the gross-up loan approach, you don't get the refund, the lender does.

Another way to get the gross-up result is to increase your regular RRSP contribution to the appropriate gross-up amount and have your employer adjust your withholding taxes so you do not get a refund.

Gross-up amounts for different tax rates are shown in the table.

By appropriately reducing the amount of taxes withheld by her employer by $1,000, Anne could contribute $2,000 a year on a monthly basis. She would also eliminate the possibility of spending the refund because she wouldn't get a refund.

A third way of getting the gross-up result occurs when you make an RRSP contribution to reduce the taxes that you owe. Here again, no refund is generated that could potentially be spent.

Math Details

The total RRSP contribution produced by the gross-up approach can be calculated by dividing the after-tax amount by one minus the tax rate. For example, with a 50% tax rate, 1.0 minus 0.5 is 0.5. $1,000 divided by one-half is $2,000, meaning that $1,000 after-tax can be grossed-up to a $2,000 RRSP contribution.

RRSP Contribution from $1,000 After-Tax

Refund Strategy	25% Tax	40% Tax	50% Tax
Spend Refund	$1,000	$1,000	$1,000
Reinvest Refund	$1,250	$1,400	$1,500
Gross-Up Refund	$1,333	$1,667	$2,000

Many people set up monthly "pay yourself first" RRSP plans. It is important to note that unless your current monthly contribution is grossed-up the right amount as shown in the table, having your employer withhold less tax does not increase your RRSP fund at all. Simply reducing your withholding taxes amounts to getting your RRSP refund back a little bit each pay period instead of all at once when you file your taxes.

Note that the gross-up refund strategy results in no loan outstanding and is different from the following two strategies where a larger loan is paid off over one or more years.

4: Top-up loan. The fourth refund strategy is to use a short-term RRSP loan to "top-up" your annual RRSP contribution to the maximum. If Anne's RRSP room was $5,000 and she had $1,000 available, she could borrow the extra $4,000. Her $2,500 refund would not pay off all of the loan. RRSP top-up loans are small and normally paid off within a year.

5: Catch-up loan. The fifth refund strategy involves using a larger "catch-up" loan that might take 10 years or more to repay. Borrowing and immediately investing a larger amount might allow you to catch-up on unused RRSP contribution room, at least temporarily.

Small top-up loans are generally accepted as a sound financial planning strategy. Using larger RRSP catch-up loans is really a new, different form of leverage where the contribution is tax deductible, but not the interest expense.

Evaluating RRSP Catch-Up Loans

Now the merits of the catch-up RRSP strategy can be compared to the other strategies where a loan is not used. Because the catch-up strategy applies more to middle-income Canadians who do not maximize their RRSPs every year, let's consider the case of Bob, who is well into the 40% tax bracket.

Bob has $20,000 of unused RRSP contribution room available. By taking out a $20,000 RRSP catch-up loan, he will get a refund of 40% of $20,000 or $8,000. This refund is immediately paid against the loan, reducing the balance to $12,000. Assuming an 8% interest expense, the remaining $12,000 can be paid off over 10 years with after-tax annual payments of $1,656.

If Bob can commit to investing at least this amount in each of the next 10 years, even during his lowest income periods, he can consider four RRSP approaches. He could use $1,656 of after-tax annual cashflow to pay off the $12,000 remaining on a catch-up loan, allowing him to get $20,000 growing in his RRSP right away. Alternatively, he could use the same after-tax cashflow and invest it into RRSPs each year, with the refund either spent, reinvested, or grossed-up.

If he contributes $1,656 into an RRSP and the 40% refund, his annual contribution totals $2,318. For someone in the 40% tax bracket, $1,656 of after-tax cashflow can be grossed-up to $2,760 per year.

The table summarizes the RRSP value for each strategy after 10 years, when the loan is paid off completely, assuming that Bob can borrow at 8% interest. Since no one knows what Bob's RRSP returns will be in the future, the strategies are evaluated for a range of returns, including returns that are higher, lower, and matching the 8% cost of borrowing. Although the results for other interest rates, tax brackets, returns, and time horizons will vary, the general conclusions still apply.

As the table shows, choosing the most effective RRSP refund strategy makes a big difference, regardless of the actual RRSP returns achieved.

RRSP Catch-Up Loan Analysis			
RRSP Value After 10 Years, 8% Interest, 40% Tax			
Return	Catch-Up Loan $20,000	Spend Refund $1,656/yr	Reinvest Refund $2,318/yr	Gross-Up Refund $2,760/yr
0%	20,000	16,560 (-17%)	23,180 (16%)	27,600 (38%)
4%	29,610	20,680 (-30%)	28,950 (-2%)	34,460 (16%)
8%	43,180	25,910 (-40%)	36,270 (-16%)	43,180 (0%)
12%	62,120	32,550 (-48%)	45,560 (-27%)	54,240 (-13%)

Evaluation of $20,000 Catch-Up loan at 8% interest. 40% tax refund reduces loan to $12,000, paid off over 10 years with after-tax payments of $1,656/yr. Compared against investing $1,656/yr annually with refunds spent, reinvested for contribution of $2,318/yr, or grossed-up to $2,760/yr. Figures in brackets show the percentage increase relative to the Catch-Up strategy. Source: *Talbot's Leverage Professional* software.

When RRSP Returns Match the Cost of Borrowing

When RRSP returns average 8%, matching the 8% interest rate charged on the loan, the catch-up strategy produces $43,180, the same benefit as making annual contributions with the refunds grossed-up. Disciplined investors who reinvest all of the refunds would end up with $36,270, or 16% less.

If Bob's normal RRSP strategy was to invest annually and spend the refunds, he would have $25,910 in his RRSP after 10 years. This is 40% less than if he had committed to the catch-up loan and used the same after-tax cashflow to get $20,000 growing in his RRSP from day one.

When RRSP Returns Exceed the Cost of Borrowing

As you might expect, when returns exceed the cost, you benefit from borrowing to get more money compounding sooner. With 12% returns, investing annually with the refunds spent produces $32,550, 48% less than the catch-up strategy. The best annual approach of grossing-up every refund produces $54,240, 13% less than the $62,120 that results by committing to a catch-up loan.

We can conclude that when returns match or exceed the cost of borrowing, the catch-up strategy is at least as good as any of the annual approaches, even the best grossed-up strategy.

When RRSP Returns Are Less Than the Cost of Borrowing

Many investors will be surprised to discover that the catch-up loan strategy often makes sense even when returns are substantially lower than the cost of borrowing.

Consider RRSP returns averaging only 4%, half of the 8% interest expense on the loan. If Bob invests annually and spends the refunds, he will have $20,680 in his RRSP after 10 years. If he is more committed to his retirement goal and reinvests the refunds, he will produce $28,950. If he uses the catch-up strategy, he will have $29,610, slightly more than if he reinvests *every* penny of every refund for *each* of the 10 years. Very few people have the discipline to do that. Only by grossing-up each of the 10 years could Bob end up slightly (16%) ahead of the catch-up approach.

Commitment is the Key

Even if returns are lower than the cost of borrowing, the catch-up loan approach can be best because it forces a higher level of commitment to your retirement goal. While Bob may *intend* to reinvest or gross-up the refunds obtained from contributing to his RRSP every year for 10 years, the loan locks in his commitment.

Once started, the loan becomes a *forced savings* plan, like a mortgage, that is not likely to be stopped. As long as you can handle the payments during the lowest income years, the forced discipline of an investment loan is often better than an automatic "pay yourself first" plan that can easily be suspended.

Each refund strategy essentially equates to different levels of commitment to your retirement goal. Financial success is more dependent on your behaviour as a consumer and investor, than choosing good investments. If your retirement goal is important to you, you will want to evaluate the most effective way for you to achieve it.

Truly disciplined investors do not need the forced commitment of a catch-up loan. Those who acknowledge their tendency to procrastinate or become distracted from their retirement goal might benefit from the forced discipline of making payments on a catch-up loan.

The real benefit of the catch-up loan strategy is the forced higher level of commitment that produces a larger RRSP fund in almost all cases, even when returns are below the cost of borrowing. This forced discipline can protect investors from the temptation to spend the refunds or suspend RRSP contributions.

Traditional Leverage Outside of RRSPs

Having addressed borrowing for RRSPs, the remainder of this *Talbot's Summary Booklet* covers the key issues of traditional leverage, or borrowing to invest outside of RRSPs.

How Investors Can Leverage

Leveraging investments can be accomplished in many ways, sometimes without even realizing it. As pointed out, using a mortgage to buy a house is leveraging.

Sources of Investment Loans

■ **Personal loans.** Banks, trust companies, and credit unions all offer personal loans that can be used for any purpose, including investments. Personal loans can be secured, or unsecured. With secured loans, the lender has access to some form of collateral, anything of value like a car or investments, to protect them from the possibility that the loan won't be repaid. Because the lender's risk is low, secured loans charge a lower interest rate than unsecured loans where no collateral is pledged.

■ **Lines of credit.** Lenders also offer lines of credit, which allow you to borrow any amount up to a predefined limit at any time. Lines of credit are more flexible than loans, allowing you to pay for money only when you need it.

Most secured lines of credit offer the option of paying only the interest expense, without paying down any of the principal. This keeps the payments as low as possible, but the loan never gets paid off. They can be secured, perhaps by your home, or unsecured. Home equity loans or lines of credit are generally the cheapest source of financing available, often at prime.

> **Definition**
>
> The prime lending rate is the lowest rate generally charged to the bank's best customers. It is the benchmark that most floating rate loans are based on.

■ **Investment loans.** Loans specifically set up for investing are available from most conventional lenders as well as some insurance and fund companies. There are a wide variety of programs available where existing non-registered investments are usually held by the lender as collateral for 1:1, 2:1, or even 3:1 loans.

With a 2:1 loan, the lender will loan up to $2 for every $1 that the investor provides as collateral. If you have $10,000 of investments, you could borrow up to $20,000 with a 2:1 loan. A 1:1 loan, where the loan matches the amount you invest, is more conservative than a 2:1 loan, and generally has a lower risk of a *margin call*.

For qualified investors, many lenders also provide 100% financing for investment loans, where no additional collateral is required. The investments purchased with the loan are held by the lender, and the loan is usually paid off over a term of 5 to 20 years to gradually reduce the lender's, and investor's, risk.

■ **Margin accounts.** Margin accounts are special accounts with a brokerage firm that allow you to purchase investments on credit and pay for only part of the investment at the time of the purchase.

> **Definition**
>
> A *margin call* occurs when your lender demands more collateral to protect a leveraged investment that has dropped in value.
>
> If you do not provide additional cash or other investments, some or all of the leveraged investments could be sold, generally at a loss, to reduce the amount of the loan.

Interest can be paid on an ongoing basis, as with investment loans, or deferred and charged to your account. *Margin* refers to the amount of the purchase price that the investor pays, not the amount that is borrowed from the brokerage firm. If the value of the margined investment drops too much, you will face a margin call, and be forced to increase the margin in the account.

Example: After watching his buddies get great one-year returns in technology stocks, Marc decided that he should get a piece of the action. To magnify his returns further, Marc used a margin account to purchase $10,000 worth of a few speculative technology stocks.

In this case, the brokerage firm lent Marc 50%, so Marc only had to pay $5,000 up front.

A few months later, the stocks dropped 40% from $10,000 to $6,000 and Marc received a margin call. Not leveraging conservatively with a diversified, long-term plan, Marc got scared and cashed out. He lost $4,000 plus $200 in interest.

If Marc had not margined and only invested $5,000, the 40% drop would have produced a smaller loss of $2,000.

■ **RRSP-linked loans.** Many people have almost all of their voluntary savings in RRSPs. Technically, RRSPs cannot be used as collateral or they become taxable. This means that many people have very little non-registered investments that could be used as collateral to secure an investment loan.

To address this, some lenders provide RRSP-linked loans that allow you to borrow without having home equity or non-registered investments. With a self-directed RRSP administered by the lender, you can borrow an amount up to the value of the RRSP for non-registered investing. This would allow you to borrow up to $50,000 if you had $50,000 in RRSPs.

■ **RRSP loans.** Loans for RRSP investments are available almost everywhere. While generally restricted to small 1-year "top-up" loans in the past, larger "catch-up" loans are now available.

Interest-Only versus Term Loans

An interest-only loan is like renting money. If you have a $100,000 loan charging 10% interest and the payments are interest-only, then the annual cost, or rent, is 10% of $100,000, or $10,000 a year. The balance of the loan stays constant over time.

Term loans, where the balance is amortized or paid off over time are more conservative than interest-only loans. Since each payment is a blend of interest and loan reduction, fewer dollars can be leveraged with the same cashflow. Also, the loan balance, and thus the amount leveraged, decreases with each payment until the loan is completely paid off at the end of the term.

With an interest-only loan, a part or all of the investment must be cashed in all at once to pay off the loan. There is the risk is that the markets might not be up when you retire, perhaps forcing you to sell at a bad time. In addition, capital gains taxes will also be triggered unnecessarily.

> **Note**
>
> Because they are more conservative, term loans are a good way for beginners to get started with leverage, and a great way for near-retirees to exit the strategy when they retire and their ability to finance the loan ends.

A term loan is gradually retired or paid off without triggering taxes and avoids the concern about short-term market fluctuations.

What Lenders Require

Borrowing to invest is a strategy that is not available to all investors. Until you have sufficient cashflow and/or collateral, you should not consider leverage and will have a difficult time qualifying for a loan.

Some lenders automatically approve small investment loans up to certain limits, especially for RRSP investing. Beyond modest amounts, lenders will check to see that you have the capacity to repay the loan, and/or collateral to protect the lender in the event that you do not.

Lenders take a close look at your Total Debt Service Ratio, or TDSR, to assess your ability to repay a debt. Your TDSR is the ratio of your gross income needed to make the required payments on all of your debts, including mortgages, car loans, credit cards, and lines of credit. The maximum TDSR that most lenders will allow is about 40%. This means that your total debt payments should not take more than 40% of your gross income.

What Investments Can be Leveraged

If you borrow to invest in RRSPs, you can invest in any RRSP-eligible investment. On the non-registered side, some of the many types of investments that can be leveraged are described below.

■ Canada Savings Bonds. Canadians borrow to invest when they purchase CSBs through a payroll savings plan. These conservative investments guarantee your original investment and a fixed rate of return. The interest expense is tax deductible even though there is little chance that the investment return is higher than the cost of borrowing.

■ Mutual funds. Mutual funds are the most popular approach for Canadians to invest in a wide variety of markets in a diversified way, managed by professional money managers. There are many types of mutual funds with varying objectives, income, and tax treatments. Growth or equity mutual funds invest in dozens of stocks with the general objective of producing above average long-term returns.

Global equity funds can take advantage of opportunities anywhere in the world. Investing in several global equity funds generally increases a Canadian investor's diversification, thus reducing economic, political, and currency risks. Additionally, global equity funds have historically produced long-term average annual returns 2-3% higher than Canadian equity funds.

Investors must realize that there are periods when equities or stocks are not the best asset class to own. However, lenders always charge a higher interest rate than the returns available from cash or bond investments.

Example: When the prime lending rate was 7.5%, the highest GIC return was 6.15%, while 30-year Canada bonds yielded 5.88%. Borrowing at 7.5% or higher to earn fully taxable interest income at a lower rate is not profitable.

In the long run, equities are the only asset class that have the potential to produce average returns that are at least as high as the interest expense paid on an investment loan.

These factors are some of the reasons why diversifying into several global equity funds is recommended as part of a conservative leverage strategy.

■ **Segregated funds.** Segregated funds, or seg funds, are the insurance industry's version of mutual funds with some additional features. Most seg funds guarantee that the investor will get at least 100% of their original investment at death, and at least 75% after 10 years. Seg funds are sometimes labeled *protected funds* or *guaranteed funds* and offer unique benefits, particularly when used with long-term leveraging.

The reset feature allows investors to reset the contract and have the guarantee based on the current higher investment value at the end of a new 10-year period. This allows you to lock in some of your profits.

Seg funds also offer potential creditor protection that may be important to business owners, and have certain estate planning benefits, including the ability to reduce probate fees.

Seg funds charge slightly higher management fees to cover the guarantees. But knowing the worst-case scenario before you start might provide some financial and emotional security and help you stay invested during down markets. Being guaranteed that your investment won't lose value at death makes seg funds attractive to older investors who don't leverage, and even more important to those who do borrow to invest.

■ **Stocks.** Stocks or shares of a corporation are easiest to leverage by using a margin account with a brokerage firm. Buying on margin allows you to pay as little as 30% of the purchase price, with the rest borrowed. Because individual stock prices generally fluctuate more and are less diversified than mutual funds, investors using margin accounts need to accept the greater risk with this method of leveraging.

■ **Bonds.** Bonds provide a predictable interest income, and a predictable return if held to maturity. Government bonds are fully guaranteed, and thus are a lower risk than other investments, but provide a limited return. The price of real bonds, unlike CSBs, fluctuates and a capital gain or loss can result if they are sold before the bond matures

■ **Real estate**. Borrowing by taking out a mortgage to buy a home is a form of leveraging. Any increase in the value of your principal residence is tax-free and the interest expense is not usually tax deductible. Fortunately, there is a way to make your mortgage interest deductible, as shown later.

If you borrow to buy a rental property that has a reasonable expectation of profit, the interest will be deductible and any gains on the property are taxable.

The Mechanics of Leverage

Borrowing to invest is fundamentally different from unleveraged investing in two ways. Mathematically, leverage magnifies returns and offsets the breakeven point.

Unlike conventional investing, there is a cost to leveraging — the after-tax interest expense — that must be covered before you profit. The minimum return that must be earned before you start making money is called the *breakeven point*. With unleveraged investing, the breakeven point is 0% and any positive return is profitable. When leveraging, if you earn a 4% return and the breakeven point is 5%, you have actually lost money even though the investment earned a positive return.

With leverage, any return less than the breakeven point is a bad return. Thus, it is important to properly understand the breakeven point because it mathematically defines the risk of the strategy, and the return that the investor needs to start benefiting from the strategy.

It is easiest to illustrate and understand the concepts of the magnification effect and breakeven point using a simplified 1-year example. Note that leveraging for short-term periods is gambling, not investing, and is not recommended. The following short-term examples are intended to make it easy to understand how the mechanics of leveraging work. Then a more realistic long-term example will be examined.

Readers who do not enjoy detailed math can review the highlighted conclusions and skip ahead to the next section. The detailed, step-by-step analysis of simple, 1-year examples allow you to come to the conclusions on your own. This is important to truly understand the concept for yourself, and to not blindly trust someone else's explanation.

Leverage Magnifies Returns

Let's say that Sue borrows and invests $10,000 for a one-year period. Depending on when and how she borrows the money, she might be able to borrow and pay 9, 8, or even 7% interest. But to be conservative and to keep the math simple, let's assume her cost of borrowing is 10%.

If she paid 10% interest on $10,000 for one year, Sue's interest expense for that year would be 10% of $10,000 or $1,000. This is her before-tax cost of borrowing. If she invests the money *outside* of an RRSP, the interest expense is generally

> **Fact**
>
> The prime interest rate in Canada has averaged about 7.4% over the last 64 years.

tax deductible, as a carrying charge on line 221 of her tax return. For simplicity, let's assume Sue is in a 50% tax bracket, which means that the $1,000 interest expense deduction produces a tax refund of $500.

So Sue's before-tax interest expense is $1,000 and after getting the $500 refund, her after-tax cost of borrowing for the year is $500. Note that Sue's expense for the year is $500, not $10,000. She commits $500 annually to control $10,000 of the lender's money.

One way to think of leverage is as a "black box" or a machine that magnifies returns and offsets the breakeven point. If Sue puts $500 into the black box, she only benefits when she gets out at least $500.

In this example, Sue's before-tax cost of borrowing is 10%, but her after-tax cost of borrowing is only 5%. This is the breakeven point. Until Sue earns an *after-tax* return of 5% or higher, she's actually losing money.

What type of investment can generate an after-tax return of 5% or higher? Outside of an RRSP, it is important to focus on after-tax returns. An 8% GIC would not even be enough because, in the 50% tax bracket, the after-tax return would only be 4%.

Depending on when you measure, long-term average returns for Canadian equity funds are around 10%. Outside of RRSPs, foreign-content limits don't restrict us to the Canadian market. Long-term returns for global equity funds have historically averaged 12 to 13%.

Example of Positive Magnification

For an example of positive magnification, let's assume a conservative equity fund return of 10% and calculate the net after-tax gain, to compare against the after-tax cost.

If Sue earns a before-tax return of 10% on the $10,000 invested, she has gained $1,000. In an equity fund, most of the return is a capital gain, with perhaps some dividends. In 2000, the *capital gains inclusion rate* dropped to 50%, meaning that only half of the capital gains are taxable.

For our simplified illustration, we'll assume that all of the return is a capital gain. Half of the $1,000 gain is taxable, or $500. In a 50% tax bracket, half of $500, or $250, is lost to taxes. Therefore, if Sue gains $1,000 and loses $250 to taxes, she is left with an after-tax gain of $750.

To summarize, for the one-year time period, Sue's after-tax cost is $500 and her after-tax gain is $750. Gaining $750 from $500 in one year equates to a 50% return on her $500 investment, but not on the $10,000 leveraged. Sue paid $500 to leverage $10,000 and gain $750, for a net after-tax gain of $250.

In this case, by using other people's money and the tax laws, Sue has leveraged, or more accurately, magnified a 10% before-tax return into a 50% after-tax return on her $500 interest payment.

Example of Negative Magnification

Now let's look at the other side of the coin and assume that a year later Sue's investment doesn't make any money and doesn't lose any either — in other words a 0% return. Of course, things can get a lot worse than this, but the math in this case is easy and illustrates the downside well enough.

On the cost side, nothing changes. She still pays $1,000 in interest, which after the tax deduction costs the same $500. On the investment side, Sue gains 0% of $10,000, or zero. For the year, she's put $500 after-tax into the black box and received nothing back.

When you invest any amount of money, and get none of it back, all of your money is gone. Mathematically, "all" is defined as 100%. "All gone" is defined as *minus* 100%. In this case, leverage has magnified a 0% before-tax return into a minus 100% after-tax return. Obviously, if Sue sold for any reason when the investment had a negative return, her leveraged return would be even worse. Sue paid $500 to leverage $10,000 which gained nothing, for a net after-tax loss of $500.

Leverage Magnifies Returns
$10,000 Interest-Only Loan for 1 Year, 50% Tax

10% Interest Cost		**10% Investment Gain**	
$1,000	Before-Tax Interest	$1,000	Before-Tax Gain
- $500	Tax Deduction (50%)	- $250	Tax (50% x $1,000 x 50%)
$500	After-Tax Cost	$750	After-Tax Gain

0% Gain: $0 Before-Tax Gain - $0 Tax = $0 After-Tax Gain

Magnification: 10% return: Turning $500 into $750 is a 50% after-tax return

0% return: Turning $500 into $0 is a –100% after-tax return

The breakeven point is the return where you *start* to make money.   In this example, Sue has spent $500 after-tax, and thus the breakeven point is the return that produces a net after-tax gain of $500.   Since she lost $500 with a 0% return, and gained $750 with a 10% return, the breakeven return is between 0% and 10%.   In this example, with a 10% interest expense, the breakeven point is 6.7%, less than the 10% interest expense.

Now let's illustrate how returns are magnified when using an investment loan to add to an investor's original investment.   This shows the effect of using a margin account or a 1:1 loan.   The 2:1 loan, where the lender loans two dollars for every dollar of collateral, magnifies returns slightly more than shown in the following simplified example.

Magnification With 1:1 Loan
$10,000 1:1 Loan for 1 Year, 10% Interest, 50% Tax

	10% Gain			**10% Loss**	
$10,000	Original Investment		$10,000	Original Investment	
+ $10,000	1:1 Investment Loan		+ $10,000	1:1 Investment Loan	
$20,000	Total Investment		$20,000	Total Investment	
+ $2,000	10% Return		- $2,000	-10% Return	
$22,000	Value After 1 Year		$18,000	Value After 1 Year	
- $10,000	Pay off loan		- $10,000	Pay off loan	
- $500	Tax (50% x $2,000 x 50%)		- $0	Tax (no tax on loss)	
- $500	Interest Cost [1]		- $500	Interest Cost [1]	
$11,000	Net After-Tax Value		$7,500	Net After-Tax Value	

10% before-tax return (7.5% after-tax) magnified to a 10% after-tax return [2]   **-10% before-tax return (-10% after-tax) magnified to a –25% after-tax loss [3]**

1: $10,000 loan x 10% interest = $1,000 before-tax - 50% deduction = $500 after-tax
2: Turning the original $10,000 into $11,000 is a gain of 10%
3: Turning the original $10,000 into $7,500 is a loss of 25%

Example: Sue has $10,000 to invest and takes out a 1:1 interest-only investment loan.   With the $10,000 loaned to her, Sue's total investment is $20,000.   With a 10% interest expense, her annual after-tax interest on the $10,000 loan is the same $500 as before.

If a year later the investment gained 10%, the $20,000 would be worth $22,000.   The tax on the $2,000 gain is 50% x $2,000 x 50% or $500.   After paying off the $10,000 loan and deducting the $500 interest expense and $500 tax, she is left with a net after-tax amount of $11,000 ($22,000 - $10,000 - $500 - $500). Using the 1:1 loan, Sue has leveraged her original $10,000 into $11,000 after one year, a gain of 10%. Here, leverage has magnified a 10% before-tax return (7.5% after-tax return) into a 10% after-tax return.

If Sue's investment loses 10%, the $20,000 is worth only $18,000 ($20,000 - $2,000) a year later. There is no tax on the capital loss. After paying off the $10,000 loan and deducting the $500 interest expense, she is left with only $7,500 ($18,000 - $10,000 - $500). This is 25% less than she started with. In this case, leveraging has magnified a -10% before-tax return (-10% after-tax) into a 25% after-tax loss.

Note that if any of the capital loss can be used to offset other capital gains, the after-tax loss is reduced.

Leveraged vs. Unleveraged Equities

Investors with available cashflow and the capacity to borrow should evaluate whether they are better off investing a small amount each year or using the same after-tax cashflow to rent a larger amount that can be invested immediately.

Unfortunately, this analysis is not as straightforward as evaluating the merits of RRSP catch-up loans. Although the cost of borrowing and the return on investment are the two key parameters in any leverage analysis, several additional factors must be taken into account to accurately model traditional leverage outside of RRSPs.

For example, to ignore taxable distributions and assume pure deferred growth like RRSPs is a common oversimplification that makes leverage look better than it really is. This is one of the reasons that anyone trying to reproduce the non-registered analysis will generally find that these projections are lower than expected. The other reason is that many leverage illustrations do not account for the fact that $120,000 might have to be withdrawn to pay off a $100,000 loan, after accounting for the capital gains taxes that are triggered.

Due to the complexity of the math, financial calculators cannot determine the before-tax value of a generic non-registered investment at some point in the future. Sophisticated financial software is required.

For this reason, many illustrations of leverage and most software programs take shortcuts to make the analysis easier but less accurate. They often illustrate only 1-year comparisons, as we have done earlier for simplicity, or do not properly account for all of the relevant parameters.

When there are potentially hundreds of thousands of dollars that can be gained or lost based on accurately identifying the best strategy, it is critical to be as objective and compre-hensive in the evaluation as possible to arrive at the correct conclusions.

It is important to realize that, like any analysis in financial planning, the results are totally dependent on the assumptions used. Inaccurate assessment or understanding of any parameter can lead to "garbage in, garbage out", and thus the wrong conclusions.

All of the analysis prepared for this booklet was prepared using *Talbot's Leverage Professional* software, developed after years of analyzing and educating investors and advisors on *conservative leverage*. To evaluate a free trial version of the software, visit www.TalbotStevens.com.

WARNING!

Although some sophisticated investors might be able to use *Talbot's Leverage Professional* software to evaluate the merits of leveraging for their own unique situation, it is recommended that investors deal with a professional financial advisor who properly understands how to use this software or something similar. Misinterpretation of a single input or result could lead to the use of leverage in a manner that does not benefit you.

Assumptions

Unless otherwise specified, the following assumptions are used for *all* non-registered analysis. It is important to keep these assumptions in mind when interpreting any results, and to remember that each individual's situation will generally be different.

■ **Type of loan**: interest-only. The investor's cashflow "rents" money that is invested. Making interest-only payments, the loan balance never decreases until the end of the savings period, when enough funds are cashed in to pay off the loan and any capital gains taxes that are triggered.

■ **Interest rate**: 9%. The highest interest rate that any leveraged investor should pay is prime + 2%, with most paying closer to prime + 1%. Using home equity as collateral, the rate can be as low as prime or below.

The prime interest rate in Canada has averaged about 7.4% over the last 64 years. With expectations of low inflation and interest rates for the future, a 9% average cost of borrowing should prove to be conservative.

■ **Tax rate**: 40%. To show how the strategy works for middle-income Canadians, a 40% tax rate is used. As you would expect, those facing higher tax rates get larger tax deductions and benefit even more from leveraging than shown here.

■ **Saving period**: 10 years. This is the minimum investment period for responsible leveraging. Investing longer lowers the breakeven point, reduces the risks, and increases the benefits of leverage.

■ **Loan amount**: $50,000. This amount can be borrowed by investing about the same amount as the average RRSP contribution of $4,400. Results can easily be halved for more conservative leverage programs, or doubled for those who can leverage $100,000. Regardless of the actual amount leveraged, the relative increase or decrease from leveraging will be the same.

■ **Annual investment**: $2,700 a year, or $225 a month, after-tax. At 9% interest, borrowing $50,000 costs $4,500 a year in interest. After a 40% tax deduction, the after-tax investment is $2,700 per year.

■ **Type of investment**: (global) equity funds, or a similar diversified investment like segregated funds or stocks that produce mostly deferred capital gains, with the potential for dividend and interest income.

■ **Tax-efficiency**: 30% of returns are distributed annually. To be more realistic and conservative, all non-registered projections assume that 30% of the before-tax returns are distributed and taxable annually, mostly as capital gains. This accounts for reasonable distributions from mutual fund managers and a minor amount of buying and selling by the investor.

Any analysis that assumes pure deferred capital gains with no annual distributions is showing the best theoretical case and overstates the benefits that most leveraging investors will realize. However, there are some ways equity investors can invest more tax-efficiently, which can make a real difference outside of RRSPs.

Some mutual funds have historically had no or low distributions. Also, a few fund companies have a special class of corporate shares that defer the tax on all gains until the investor cashes in. For someone in a 50% tax bracket, these tax-efficient funds can potentially give the investor an *additional* $100,000 per $100,000 leveraged over 20 years, relative to "typical" mutual funds, where 30% of returns are distributed annually.

■ **Capital gains inclusion rate**: 50%. In 2000, the taxable portion of capital gains was dropped from 75% to 50%, increasing the benefit of borrowing to get more money invested earlier.

Note that the preceding assumptions represent the minimum conditions suggested for leveraging responsibly. These assumptions are intentionally chosen to understate the benefits of leveraging and minimize the potential for unrealistic expectations. Investors who are either in a higher tax bracket, invest for more than 10 years, or invest in more tax-efficient equities should realize an even greater benefit from leveraging than presented here.

Let's assume that Joe is an investor with the assumptions above, and use his situation to illustrate how leverage compares to an unleveraged approach. To show all possible outcomes, the net results for a range of returns are calculated.

> ## Note
>
> All leverage results show the *net* investment value after paying off the loan and associated taxes, not the total amount including the loan.

Joe has at least $2,700 a year that he can invest into equity mutual funds. Alternatively, he could use the same cashflow to borrow and invest $50,000. Paying 9% interest on a $50,000 loan costs $4,500 before the 40% tax deduction. Joe's after-tax investment is $2,700 a year, or $225 a month.

If Joe averages 0% returns, the interest payments made to borrow someone else's money gains nothing. The $50,000 borrowed is worth the same $50,000 after 10 years, leaving Joe with no net gain. If Joe had not leveraged, his investment of $2,700 a year over 10 years would be worth $27,000.

The breakeven point is the return where the net amount gained equals the net cost or amount invested. This is the return that nets $27,000, the total amount invested, after paying off the loan and associated capital gains taxes. In this case, the breakeven point is 5.1%, or a little more than half of the cost of borrowing, dispelling the fourth myth.

Leveraged vs. Unleveraged Equities
Net Value After Invest $2,700/yr for 10 Years, 40% Tax

Return	No Leverage	Leverage	$ Increase	% Increase
0%	27,000	0	-27,000	-100%
3%	30,700	14,100	-16,600	-54%
5.1%	33,650	27,000	-6,650	-20%
6.3%	35,500	35,500	0	0%
9%	40,000	58,100	18,100	45%
12%	45,700	90,100	44,400	97%
15%	52,400	130,700	78,300	149%

The table shows the net before-tax value when someone in a 40% tax bracket **invests $2,700/year** for 10 years. At **9% interest**, this cashflow **leverages $50,000**. 30% of equity fund returns taxable annually. 50% of capital gains taxable. Source: *Talbot's Leverage Professional* software from www.TalbotStevens.com.

Leveraging and not leveraging produce the same net value of $35,500 when returns average 6.3%. This is the minimum return needed for Joe to benefit from leveraging. Thus, the "Better Than" return is 6.3%, or about two-thirds of the cost of borrowing. This dispels the fifth myth.

Having determined that before-tax annual returns need to average 6.3% to benefit from leveraging, you should ask yourself, *"Can I reasonably expect diversified equity returns to average at least 6.3% over a decade or more?"* If the answer is yes, then it makes sense to learn more about the risks of leveraging and how to implement responsibly. Otherwise, stick to unleveraged investing.

If Joe's returns equal the 9% interest expense, he would have $40,000 without leveraging, and a net value of $58,100 by borrowing to invest. In this case, leveraging increases Joe's retirement funds by about 45%.

If Joe's returns are 12%, slightly less than the historical average for global equity funds, leverage is 97% better than the unleveraged approach, effectively doubling Joe's retirement fund. Averaging a 9% interest expense and 12% equity returns, leveraging for 10 years could increase Joe's investments by an extra $44,400, per $50,000 leveraged.

Leverage Risk Decreases Over Time

One of my criteria for conservative leverage is that you should invest for a minimum of 8 to 10 years. This is strongly recommended because the risk of not benefiting from leverage decreases over time for two reasons.

The first reason is that the breakeven point decreases over time, even for interest-only borrowing. This occurs because the cost of borrowing stays constant, while investments increase in value over time.

We have already seen how the breakeven point in our simple 1-year example was 6.7%, when the interest expense was 10%, but dropped to 5.1% in the 10-year projection when the cost of borrowing was 9%. The breakeven point dropped from two-thirds of the cost of borrowing to a little over half of the cost of borrowing.

Understanding the real breakeven point and how it decreases over time dispels the fourth myth. The actual breakeven point depends on the length of the investment period, the tax rate, and the type of investment, as we will demonstrate below.

The second reason that the risk of not profiting with leverage decreases over time is that the longer you hold a diversified equity investment, the more likely the compounded return will be near the long-term average of 10 to 12%.

In his book, *Risk is a Four Letter Word*, George Hartman reveals that in a recent 42-year period, 1-year returns in the Canadian stock market ranged from a low of –28% to a high of 51%. However, when stocks were held for 10 years, returns ranged from a low of 4% to 18%. When held for 25 years, the historical compounded returns ranged from 7% to 12%. Clearly, holding equity investments longer decreases the volatility in the returns achieved and increases the probability of returns being above the critical "Better Than" return.

The Most Important Parameters

As you would expect, the most important parameters affecting the profitability of leveraging are the investment returns and the interest rate on the loan.

The minimum return needed for leverage to be better depends on other factors, including the tax bracket, time horizon, type and tax-efficiency of the investments, type of leverage, and capital gains inclusion rate.

Impact of Tax Rate

The most critical number for indicating whether leverage will benefit or hurt an investor is the "Better Than" return — the minimum return needed for leverage to produce more than not leveraging.

Minimum Return for Leverage to be Better With a 9% Cost of Borrowing			
Years Invested	50% Tax	40% Tax	25% Tax
1	6.0%	6.7%	7.6%
5	5.8%	6.5%	7.5%
10	5.6%	6.3%	7.3%
20	5.3%	6.1%	7.2%
30	5.2%	5.9%	7.1%

Table shows the before-tax equity fund return for leverage to be better than not leveraging, assuming a 9% interest-only investment loan. 30% of returns are distributed and taxable annually. 50% of capital gains taxable. Source: *Talbot's Leverage Professional* software.

The above table shows the minimum returns needed to benefit from leveraging equity funds for different investment periods and tax brackets. The "Better Than" return is slightly lower with higher tax brackets, confirming that investors with higher tax rates are more likely to benefit from leverage than those in lower tax brackets.

Assuming a 9% cost of borrowing and investing for 20 years, those in the 50% tax bracket need average equity returns of 5.3% to benefit from interest-only leveraging. Those in a 25% tax bracket need to average 7.2% returns for leverage to be better.

Also note how the return needed to benefit decreases as the investment period increases. As a rough rule of thumb, when investing at least 10 years, returns only need to be about two-thirds of the interest expense for leveraging to benefit you. Those in the top tax bracket can benefit when earning less.

Impact of Type of Investment

The type of investment chosen has a large impact on the potential benefit of borrowing to invest.

The most profitable type of investment to leverage is one that has the potential to produce income so that the interest expense is tax deductible but has the majority of the returns in the form of deferred capital gains, as with equity mutual funds. When investing in equity funds outside of an RRSP, the tax-efficiency of the funds chosen is important.

Maximum growth occurs when all of the return is a deferred capital gain, with no taxable annual distributions. While there are a few investments that achieve this, most mutual funds have taxable distributions that reduce growth.

Again, let's use the critical "Better Than" return to illustrate the impact of the type of investment on leveraging. With Joe averaging a 9% interest expense, in the 40% tax bracket, and investing for 10 years, the minimum returns for leveraging to be better than not leveraging for various investments are as follows:

- For interest investments like Canada Savings Bonds or GICs, he will need to exceed 9%, the same as the cost of borrowing.
- For a balanced fund that is approximately 50% equities and 50% bonds, the "Better Than" return is about 7.4%.
- For regular equity funds with typical distributions, Joe needs at least 6.3% returns for leverage to be better, as shown.
- For pure deferred capital gains with no distributions, Joe needs to average only 6.1% to benefit from leveraging.

Risks of Borrowing to Invest

The two critical issues for reducing the risk of leveraging are:
- understanding thoroughly all of the pros and *cons*
- staying conservative on your cash flow, collateral, and emotions

If you can financially and, more importantly, emotionally handle the worst-case scenario, you should benefit from a properly structured leverage program. The key is to use Donald Trump's approach and "Take care of the downside, and the upside will take care of itself."

There are at least 7 leverage-related risks. Each is described below with strategies on how to minimize or eliminate them. These strategies form the basis of Talbot's Conservative Leverage Checklist, detailed in the Getting Started section.

Company Risk

Company risk is the reality that even if you invest in a solid blue chip stock, there is always the possibility that the company is "blue chip" one day and "no chip" the next, after the company unexpectedly announces bankruptcy. Confed Life and Bre-X are just a few of the recent examples.

Solutions: Company risk can be significantly reduced by **diversifying** in many different companies in several sectors of the economy. While affluent investors can do this by diversifying into a number of stocks directly, it is more practical for most investors to use **mutual funds** or **segregated funds**. Using **balanced funds** reduces exposure to one asset class and hence further lowers volatility.

Political Risk

Political risk is the concern that the government could change the rules in a way that hurts you. Any changes in the deductibility of interest for traditional non-registered leveraging, or an increase in capital gains taxes, would naturally reduce the attractiveness of borrowing to invest.

Solutions: There is no way to completely eliminate political risk. It will always exist as long as someone else can change the rules that affect you. Political risk can be minimized by **diversifying by investment strategy, diversifying geographically** with global funds, and leveraging modestly.

Market Risk

Market risk is the possibility that the entire market as a whole does not produce the expected returns. This is more of an issue with leveraged investing because the breakeven point is generally between 4 and 8%.

> **Solutions: Long-term** investing in **several globally diversified mutual funds** reduces market risk. Virtually no diversified equity fund has lost money over any 10-year period. This is why my Conservative Leverage Checklist suggests investing at least 8 to 10 years. Including some **balanced funds** also reduces market risk.
>
> **Segregated funds** guarantee that you get at least 75% of your original investment back after 10 years, or 100% upon death.

Interest Rate Risk

Interest rate risk is the possibility that interest rates may rise. Higher interest rates affect leveraged investors in several ways. A higher cost of borrowing obviously raises the breakeven point. At the same time, *short-term* stock market returns are probably going down because higher interest rates slow economic growth. Worse than these factors is the possibility that if you can no longer afford the payments on the investment loan, you may be forced to sell, probably at a bad time.

Short-term interest rates are unpredictable. What matters most to a long-term leveraged investor is the long-term relationship between the cost of borrowing and investment returns.

Although there have been periods where GICs have outperformed equities, over the last 64 years the prime interest rate in Canada has averaged 7.4%, compared to long-term total returns for the Canadian stock market of around 9 to 11%.

> **Solutions:** The risk of increasing loan costs can be reduced in several ways:
> - Stay **conservative on your cashflow**, by using a maximum of 50% of your available cashflow for leveraging.
> - Maintain **additional emergency funds**.
> - Consider **locking in the interest rate** over a longer term.
>
> Using a maximum of 50% of your available cashflow ensures that even if interest rates double, you can still handle the loan payments. Having *additional* emergency funds can help cover higher-than-expected loan costs during short-term periods of higher interest rates.

- Forced commitment towards independence. Borrowing for consumption forces a high level of commitment to paying for today's standard of living, leaving little cashflow to invest to pay for your desired standard of living in the future. Borrowing to invest forces a commitment that increases your wealth, allowing you to become more financially independent over time.

Investment Swap

If you have some investments and non-deductible debts, such as a mortgage, car loans, or credit cards, you can do an investment swap to lower your real interest costs. Investments that can be cashed without triggering capital gains taxes, like GICs, are best for investment swaps.

> **Example:** Michael has $10,000 of unregistered GICs and the balance on his car loan is $15,000. He can pay down the car balance using the $10,000 of GICs and borrow $10,000 to purchase other investments. Michael's net worth stays the same because he still owes $15,000 and has $10,000 of investments. But now the interest expense on the $10,000 investment loan is tax deductible, and probably at a lower rate, decreasing his after-tax costs.

Make Mortgage Interest Deductible

If you have non-registered investments and a mortgage, you can do an investment swap to make a portion of your mortgage interest tax deductible in the same way.

A related approach is to use home equity as collateral for a loan. Lenders will generally allow you to mortgage 75% of a home's value.

> **Example:** The Robinsons own a $200,000 home and have reduced their mortgage to $50,000. Lenders would let them borrow up to $150,000 secured by the house by increasing the mortgage or setting up a home equity line of credit up to $100,000.
>
> Practicing conservative leverage, the Robinsons borrow and invest only $50,000 of the $100,000 line of credit they are qualified for.

The big risk of using your home as collateral for an investment loan is that you could lose your house if you can't make the payments, as with any mortgage. A minor negative is that there may be appraisal and legal fees involved. If fees are charged, they are not deductible up front, but provide some tax relief later by reducing the taxable gain when you sell your investments.

Balancing these negatives are several benefits of using a conservative portion of your home equity as collateral for an investment loan.

- Home equity is often the only real collateral available for many people who have a large portion of their wealth in their home and few investments outside of RRSPs.
- The lowest interest rates are for loans secured by your home. Mortgage rates can be below prime, and home lines of credit are usually at prime.
- No risk of a margin call. Since the home, and not the investments purchased, provides the collateral for the loan, there is never a risk of a margin call no matter how much your investments fluctuate.
- Better growth prospects. Demographics suggest that real estate in most parts of the country will not appreciate the way it did in the 70s and 80s. Instead, real estate growth is predicted to be closer to inflation.

Combination RRSP-Leverage Plans

Because the interest expense deduction produces the same tax savings as an RRSP contribution, leverage can be viewed as an alternative investment strategy to RRSPs. This is important for the many Canadians looking for additional tax-saving investment strategies beyond their RRSPs.

Unregistered equities that defer most of the growth in the form of capital gains are a tax-effective strategy on their own. Capital gains grow tax-deferred like RRSPs, and are only partially taxed. With any unregistered investment, you get the amount you invested back tax-free. To also get the major RRSP benefit of tax savings, you can borrow to invest in equities and deduct the interest expense annually.

Together these factors mean that leveraging equities outside of an RRSP can be better than sheltering equities inside of RRSPs, even when returns only match the cost of borrowing.

Regardless of whether leveraging is better than RRSPs for the equity portion of your portfolio, no one knows what political or tax changes will affect a particular investment strategy 25 years from now. Most middle-income Canadians who have the majority of their voluntary savings inside RRSPs should recognize a significant, yet overlooked, risk.

Is it a safe, sound retirement planning approach to have almost all of your voluntary savings in *any* single investment strategy?

This overlooked need to diversify by strategy is a strong argument to consider leverage as a *complement* to RRSPs, by using a combination RRSP and leverage plan.

Suggestions for Combination RRSP-Leverage Plans

The following suggestions can help you design an effective combination RRSP and leverage plan.

- Leverage up to your unique definition of conservative, and then reinvest the refund back into RRSPs. Alternatively, invest in RRSPs first, and use the tax refunds to finance an investment loan.
- Shelter all interest bearing investments. This protects the least tax-efficient investments with the most powerful and flexible tax shelter.
- Leverage mostly equity investments. Inside of RRSPs, the "taxed less" and "taxed later" benefits of capital gains are lost, as well as the ability to use capital losses.

Benefits of Combination RRSP-Leverage Plans

A combination of conservatively leveraged equities outside of RRSPs, and all other investments inside of RRSPs generates the following benefits:

- Produces a balanced plan that generates tax deductions for every dollar invested, where most of the funds grow tax deferred. This combination integrates two of the most powerful and tax-efficient investment strategies available to Canadians.
- Maximizes the use of the tax refunds. Committing the refunds in advance solves a significant human behaviour threat to most retirement plans. Unfortunately, most people spend their tax refunds from RRSPs. Automatically directing the tax refunds into an alternative tax deduction strategy ensures that the refunds are "not wasted". This generates a second-generation tax refund that can be spent to allow you to enjoy today, while saving more for tomorrow.
- Diversifies by asset class, allowing significant or total tax deferral of each of the three basic asset classes: equities or stocks, bonds, and cash-like investments like GICs.
- Diversifies geographically, allowing much greater exposure to global equity markets to reduce economic, political, and currency risks while potentially increasing returns. Using a combination approach, where there are no foreign content limits on the non-registered leveraged equities, global diversification can be achieved without the slightly higher cost of RRSP clone funds.
- Diversifies by strategy, with some registered money and some unregistered. Regardless of which strategy might be best right now, do you want to have *all* of your voluntary retirement savings in *any single* strategy? Is it a safe, sound retirement planning approach to have all of your weight on any single branch of a tree?

     If the government changes the rules on any strategy, it won't hurt you as much if you don't have all of your eggs in one basket. The cancelled Seniors Benefit legislation would have significantly reduced the effectiveness of RRSPs. Some think that increased clawbacks are inevitable, possibly producing higher tax rates in retirement.

Example: Martin is in the 40% tax bracket and invests $5,000/yr into RRSPs. After recognizing the benefits of directing his refund towards his retirement and diversifying by strategy, he considers RRSP-leverage combination plans. He expects to average 10% returns over the next 14 years and then retire. For this simplified illustration, assume he borrows at 10% interest.

Current approach: Invest $5,000 a year into RRSPs and spend the refunds of $2,000 (40% of $5,000) on an international vacation. Growing at 10% for 14 years, this produces RRSPs worth about $140,000.

RRSP-Leverage combination: Invest $5,000 a year into RRSPs, as he does now, and use the $2,000 refunds to pay interest on a $20,000 investment loan. Martin is pleased to discover that the $2,000 of interest expense also generates a tax refund of $800 (40% of $2,000), which he plans to use to pay for a smaller Canadian vacation.

The RRSP contributions grow to the same $140,000. The rule of 72 tells us that at 10% growth, money doubles in value every 72/10 = 7.2 years. Thus, the $20,000 investment loan is worth $40,000 after 7 years, and $80,000 after about 14 years. After withdrawing about $24,000 to pay off the loan and associated capital gains taxes, the $20,000 investment loan adds a net value of $56,000 ($80,000 - $24,000) to Martin's retirement fund. The RRSP-leverage approach produces a total retirement fund of $196,000 (140K + 56K).

Leverage-RRSP combination: Invest $5,000 a year to pay interest on a $50,000 investment loan, and direct the $2,000 refunds into RRSPs. The $2,000 RRSP contributions generate annual tax refunds of $800 (40% of $2,000), to pay for a Canadian vacation.

The annual RRSP contributions of $2,000 grow to about $56,000. The $50,000 leveraged investment doubles twice and is worth $200,000 after 14 years. After withdrawing about $60,000 to pay off the loan and associated capital gains taxes, the $50,000 investment loan adds a net value of $140,000 ($200,000 - $60,000) to Martin's retirement fund. Thus, the Leverage-RRSP combination produces a total retirement fund of $196,000 (140K + 56K).

Decision: Being new to leveraging, Martin decides to start with the RRSP-Leverage combination and will evaluate upgrading to the Leverage-RRSP strategy in a few years after he's gained some experience. He likes the tradeoff of taking smaller vacations for the potential to add an extra $56,000 to his retirement fund.

RRSP-Leverage Combination Plans
Invest $5,000/yr, 40% Tax, 10% Interest, 10% Returns

Yr	RRSP $5K/yr into RRSP, spend $2K refunds	RRSP -Lev $5K/yr into RRSP, $2K refunds pay interest on $20K loan		Lev - RRSP $5K/yr pays interest on $50K loan, $2K refunds into RRSP	
1	$5,000/yr	$5,000/yr	$20K	$50K	$2,000/yr
-	-	-	-	-	-
-	-	-	-	-	-
7	-	-	$40K	$100K	-
-	-	-	-	-	-
-	-	-	-	-	-
14	-	-	$80K	$200K	-
			-$24K	-60K	
			(loan and taxes)	(loan and taxes)	
	———	$140K	$56K	$140K	$56K
	$140K (+Int'l Vac'n)	**$196K** (+Can. Vac'n)		**$196K** (+Can. Vac'n)	

Systematic Withdrawal Plans

If you could borrow and earn higher returns, it is theoretically possible that a portion of the annual growth could be withdrawn to totally cover the interest payments. On paper, this would be the equivalent of a self-perpetuating money making machine, where the net investment value increases on its own, without requiring any cashflow from you.

This leads some to suggest the strategy of setting up a Systematic Withdrawal Plan, or SWP, with mutual funds to automatically make the payments on an investment loan. While this approach can work, it is not recommended. Investment returns fluctuate, sometimes greatly, and if the first few years produce lower-than-average returns, the system could collapse and never recover.

Instead of expecting the loan to be self-financing from the start, a more reasonable approach is to cover the loan payments with your own cashflow until the leveraged investment has doubled in value. This builds up additional buffer that can withstand a few years of bad returns.

Although borrowing to invest can provide significant benefits, it is not for everyone. Regardless of the potential upside of borrowing to invest, the real benefits of any investment loan approach are the forced higher level of commitment to your investment goals, and the diversification by strategy.

The following Emotional Acid Test can help determine if you are emotionally ready for the potential downside of leveraging. It also helps you stay focused on the long-term plan when investments are down. The question should be considered just *before* signing for an investment loan.

Emotional Acid Test

If *my* investments drop 30% in value 3 weeks from now, I will:

- ❏ A: Want to buy more, because investments are now "on sale"
- ❏ B: Have faith and hold, committed to the long-term plan
- ❏ C: Hold somewhat nervously, questioning why I leveraged
- ❏ D: Want to sell, unable to sleep at night due to stress
- ❏ E: Insist on selling, stressed and upset with my advisor
- ❏ F: Shoot my advisor and/or educator who introduced leverage

Date	Signature	Spouse's Signature

If you answer D, E, or F, you are not ready for leveraging. If your honest answer is C, then you may want to reconsider, wait, or start with a smaller amount until you gain more confidence and understanding.

When Not to Borrow to Invest

The following guidelines outline when it is not appropriate to consider borrowing to invest.

- Leveraging is not possible until you have the capacity to borrow, facilitated by good cashflow and acceptable collateral.
- Do not borrow if you do not have solid income or cashflow that can easily support the loan payments if interest rates double.
- Never borrow out of desperation or expect to get rich quick.

- Most importantly, do not borrow until you fully understand, and can emotionally handle, the potential downside.

Implementing Conservative Leverage

The key to benefiting from leveraging is understanding and implementing responsibly. Conservative leverage only makes sense as a part of an integrated financial plan that is diversified by strategy and asset class. Leveraging aggressively is gambling, and a recipe for disaster.

While there are no guarantees, following the Conservative Leverage Checklist should significantly enhance the odds of benefiting from borrowing to invest. Each of the conditions for conservative leverage essentially addresses one or more of the leverage-related risks, and is explained in more detail below.

Talbot's Conservative Leverage Checklist

- ❏ Stay *conservative* on cash flow, collateral, and emotions
- ❏ Eliminate the risk of a margin call
- ❏ Invest long term, minimum of 8-10 years
- ❏ Diversify in several (global equity) funds
- ❏ Use a trusted advisor to help understand all pros and cons, implement, and stick to the plan

---

Stay Conservative

The best way to reduce the risk of bailing out at the worst time is to stay conservative on your cashflow, collateral, and emotions.

This means that if you think you can afford payments of $500 a month, start with $250. That way, if interest rates double, you can still handle it. Don't automatically start with the largest amount that you qualify for. Only leverage a conservative amount that can be easily handled with a portion of your available cashflow. Don't be desperate or greedy. Make it easy to handle the payments even during your lowest income periods.

It is safer to start slowly and gain some experience. As your confidence and understanding grows, your definition of conservative will expand, allowing you to comfortably leverage a little more later.

Eliminate the Risk of a Margin Call

A margin call forces you to provide more collateral. If you satisfy the margin call by investing more, you end up buying more units when the price is low. This would actually benefit you in the long term as your diversified investments recovered.

Unfortunately, most people panic when a margin call is issued, and end up selling at the worst possible time. For almost everyone, eliminating the risk of a margin call is a must. Use a loan program that guarantees no margin calls. Use collateral, like home equity, that does not fluctuate with the investments. Provide additional collateral so that a 40% drop in the market would not trigger a margin call. Do whatever it takes to avoid finding out how you would respond to the Emotional Acid Test in real life.

A critical aspect of *conservative* leverage is that you should never be in a position where you could be *forced* to sell, either due to a margin call, lack of cashflow, or to reduce emotional stress.

Invest Long Term

Be committed to investing for a minimum of 8 to 10 years. Investing long term reduces the breakeven point and hence the risk of not making money. It also increases the probability that your diversified returns will come closer to the long-term historical average, and be above the minimum needed for leverage to be better than not leveraging.

Diversify in Several Funds

Unless you have significant investments to allow effective diversification in individual stocks, mutual funds or their seg funds cousins are the easy way for most investors to diversify responsibly. With a long-term focus, a large portion should be in equities.

Using several funds, with the majority diversified globally, provides additional protection against economic, currency, and political risks while historically providing higher returns.

Use a Trusted Advisor

Most people can benefit from the expertise of a professional financial advisor for general financial planning. Getting the guidance of a trusted professional is even more important when borrowing to invest.

A good advisor will help you understand all of the pros and *cons*, implement responsibly to reduce the related risks, and help choose appropriate diversified investments. Perhaps the most important reason to work with a competent advisor is that they will help ensure that you stick to the plan, especially during tough times when the natural tendency is to self-sabotage.

5-Minute Summary

For those really busy individuals, the following 5-Minute Summary highlights the most important concepts. It also serves as a concise review.

Introduction to Borrowing to Invest

- Borrowing to invest, or leveraging, is a double-edged sword that, like a power tool, can either benefit or hurt you, depending on how you use it.
- Myth 1: Leverage is only for the wealthy. Reality: Anyone can benefit from the ideas of others, perhaps on a smaller scale.
- Myth 2: All debts are bad. Reality: Expensive consumer debt is bad. Investment debt is generally good debt that can increase wealth.
- Myth 3: Leverage is too risky for me. Reality: Most homeowners have already leveraged in a less effective way by taking out a mortgage.
- Myth 4: Returns must exceed the cost to be profitable. Reality: With investments that have some deferred capital gains, the breakeven point is lower than the interest expense, and it decreases over time.
- Myth 5: Returns must exceed the cost for leverage to be better. Reality: Leveraging equity investments can benefit the investor when returns are about two-thirds of the interest rate on the investment loan.
- The interest expense of borrowing to invest in RRSPs is not tax deductible. When borrowing to invest outside of RRSPs, the interest is generally deductible if the investment has the potential to produce income in the form of dividends or interest.

Borrowing for RRSPs

- There are at least 5 distinct RRSP refund strategies, where the refund is spent, reinvested, grossed-up, or where a top-up or catch-up loan is used. Choosing the best RRSP refund strategy can increase the size of your retirement fund by 25 to 50% or more.
- The RRSP catch-up strategy is always better when returns match or exceed the interest expense, and is generally better even when returns are as little as half of the interest expense.
- The most important benefit of any investment loan strategy is the forced savings and higher level of commitment to your goals.

Traditional Leverage Outside of RRSPs

- Leverage simply magnifies returns and offsets the breakeven point. It makes good returns better and bad returns worse.
  - With a simplified 1-year example, leveraging can magnify a 10% before-tax return into a 50% after-tax return, and a 0% before-tax return into a –100% after-tax return.
- The risk of not benefiting with leverage decreases over time. This is because, as your time horizon increases, the breakeven point drops and you increase the odds of producing diversified equity returns near the long-term average.
- When leveraging equity funds in a 40% tax bracket for 10 years:
  - Leveraging is better than not leveraging when returns are about two-thirds of the cost of borrowing.
  - Leveraging with 9% interest and averaging 12% returns produces about twice as much as possible without leveraging, adding an extra $44,400 *per* $50,000 borrowed.
- The most important parameters affecting the profitability of leverage are the investment returns and the cost of borrowing. Other important factors are the tax rate, the type and tax-efficiency of the investments, and length of time invested.

Risks of Borrowing to Invest

- The key to reducing leverage risks is understanding and implementing conservatively.
- There are at least 7 leverage-related risks, including company risk, political risk, market risk, interest rate risk, margin call risk, cashflow risk, and emotional risk.
- Investors should ask themselves if leveraging a small, conservative portion of what they are able to borrow produces more or less *total* risk than not leveraging at all.
- Following Talbot's Conservative Leverage Checklist is an effective way to reduce the risk of not benefiting from leverage.

Leveraging Strategies

- Borrow to increase wealth. Instead of paying cash for investments and borrowing at high, non-deductible rates to purchase consumer goods that depreciate quickly, borrow for investments at lower, tax-deductible rates to increase your wealth, and pay cash for consumer goods.
- If you have investments and consumer debt or a mortgage, an investment swap can make some of the interest deductible and lower your after-tax costs.

- Using home equity for leveraging eliminates the risk of a margin call and generally is the lowest-cost way to borrow.
- RRSP-leverage combination plans integrate two of the best tax-savings investment strategies, productively investing the tax refunds. The combination is also an effective way to diversify by asset class, geographically, and most importantly, by strategy.
- Setting up a Systematic Withdrawal Plan, or SWP, to finance an investment loan is not recommended until the leveraged investment has doubled in value.

Getting Started

- The best way to reduce the risk of not benefiting from leverage is to thoroughly understand the strategy and implement responsibly by following Talbot's Conservative Leverage Checklist:
  - ❑ Stay conservative on cashflow, collateral, and emotions
  - ❑ Eliminate the risk of a margin call
  - ❑ Invest a minimum of 8 to 10 years
  - ❑ Diversify into several (global equity) funds
  - ❑ Use a trusted financial advisor to help you understand the risks, choose appropriate investments, and stick to the plan

Other Products and Services

To learn more about other educational products and services, or evaluate free trial versions of our software, visit www.TalbotStevens.com.

Financial Seminars

Talbot Stevens offers a variety of employer-sponsored and public seminars. Entertaining and valuable, these workshops are an effective way to add tangible value to employees, increasing their satisfaction and commitment in the workplace. The seminars include 50 FREE copies of a *Talbot's Summary Booklet* or his book *Financial Freedom Without Sacrifice* — up to a $1,000 retail value.

Financial Freedom Without Sacrifice

Talbot Stevens' first book *Financial Freedom Without Sacrifice* shows you how to cut expenses, invest, and increase security without lowering your standard of living. Using an easy-to-read, entertaining storyline approach, readers of all ages will enjoy learning how to be a better consumer and investor — **GUARANTEED**.

"Introduction to Conservative Leverage" Pamphlet

To further help investors understand how and when the conservative use of leverage can make sense as a part of an integrated financial plan, Talbot has created an educational 12-page pamphlet on leverage that is focused on the basic, introductory issues suitable for the majority of investors.

RRSP Contribution Optimizer Software

For those who have unused RRSP contribution room, Talbot's web-based RRSP Contribution Optimizer software helps define your optimal contribution strategy, accounting for different tax brackets, clawbacks and behaviour. This unique education and analysis tool significantly benefits investors, advisors, lenders, and investment companies.

Leverage Professional Software

In minutes, you can calculate the net benefit (or loss) over a range of returns from borrowing to invest in or outside of RRSPs for your unique situation. Analysis includes RRSP catch-up loans, interest-only loans, and term loans.